Grace and Mercy
in Her Wild Hair

Grace and Mercy in Her Wild Hair

SELECTED POEMS TO THE
MOTHER GODDESS

RĀMPRASĀD SEN

Translated by
Leonard Nathan and Clinton Seely

HOHM PRESS
Prescott, Arizona
1999

Library of Congress Cataloging in Publications Data
Rāmprasād Sena, 1718-1775.
   Grace and mercy in her wild hair; selected poems to the mother
goddess / Rāmprasād Sen: translated by Leonard Nathan and Clinton
Seely.
       p.   cm.
   Originally published: Boulder, Colo : Great Eastern Book Co.
   1982
   ISBN: 0-934252-94-7
   1. Kālī (Hindu deity)--Poetry.   I. Nathan, Leonard. II. Seely,
   Clinton B. III. Title.
PK1718.R2514A28   1999
891.4'413--dc21   99-22779
                                                                          CIP

Cover design: Kim Johansen; original art by Marcus Alsop
Layout: Shukyo Lin Rainey, and Harvard Print & Copy Center

HOHM PRESS
P.O. 2501,
Prescott, AZ 86302
800-381-2700   http://www.hohmpress.com

Poems in this book have appeared before in somewhat different forms
in The San Francisco *Barque: A Gathering of Bay Area Poets;
The Malahat Review; Practices of the Wind;* and *The Likeness* by
Leonard Nathan (Thorp Springs Press, 1975.)

Published by arrangement with Shambhala Publications, Inc.,
Boston.

CONTENTS

FOREWORD
by Andrew Schelling

At the molten magnetic core of our planet, or in some tellings of it, at the base of our own spines, is a terrible burning ground of Life and Death. There, on the reclining corpse of her husband, the Mother of all things—Gaia or Tellus, Kālī or Durgā—performs a naked dance, slow and insistent as geomorphic force. While She dances, nearby flames devour the tender creatures to whom She has given birth. Vultures and feral dogs pick at the leftover corpses. It is a frightful ground to those who glimpse it, but it is the field on which the Shaktas, devotees of the Goddess, gather to worship.

Do not imagine the Shaktas to be some alienated turn-of-the-millennium cult addicted to video-game imagery. It is likely they are the inheritors of insights that reach deep into the paleolithic. What they study is the complicated mix of violent and benign forces that govern our planet. In Bengal, where the Shaktas are most numerous, they and their beliefs are called *guhya*: covered, concealed, sequestered, mysterious; underground; the hidden recess. For centuries this term has been applied to caves and grottos as well as to the female sexual organ. No wonder the Shaktas of Bengal stay underground. They have glimpsed a terrible secret. It is that the Great Mother of all beings in one of her truest moods is a shameless, naked, wilderness goddess, companioned by jackals, stoned out of her senses on blood or ganja, who performs a slow orgiastic dance while her children die.

In recent years Western cultures have learnt a great deal about their own matrilocal origins. The way has been led by feminist scholars, who have done heroic work stripping off centuries of wrong-headed social beliefs. Likewise, studies by Marija Gimbutas and others have publicized the hundreds of stone-age female fertility statuettes found across Europe and the Near East. These figurines, with their ample hips, buttocks and breasts, have begun to present a human self-image that seems both postmodern and utterly archaic. The Willendorf Venus, on display in the state museum in Vienna, has become a celebrated icon of a postmodern Europe. There are also the renowned Shila-na-gig (cunt shrines) of Ireland, as well as female sex-organ images on cave walls in the Dordogne. "The Goddess is Awake and Magic is Afoot," alertly declares a Wiccan bumper sticker.

It is unlikely however that the Goddess, the Great Mother, is to be known by the study of comparative religion (though this may tell us many interesting things), by searching out archaic amulets, or by posting a bumper sticker.

> Who knows
> What She truly is?
>
> Rāmprasād says: If She decides
> To be kind, this misery will pass.

Rāmprasād Sen (ca. 1718-1775), who lived out his days in a small village north of Calcutta, may be Her finest surviving poet. I say surviving because there is no way to retrieve the many songs to the Goddess that vanished before humans learnt to put speech into writing. Nor can anyone restore the manuscripts lost from places like monsoon India when fungus, insects, water or fire devoured them. Or those destroyed by intolerant clerics in Europe or Mesoamerica. Of what remains, there is much we are lucky to have at all. For this reason I cannot tell you with what gratitude I welcome back into print these fine translations by Leonard Nathan and Clinton Seely. Their task has been a difficult one—to move between languages as different as eighteenth-century Bengali and contemporary American English, to catch in our own tongue some of the chewable slangy quality of songs preserved "on the street" for two hundred years. And most difficult of all, to convey Rāmprasād Sen's tough, wry, wheedling, brave, and utterly vulnerable manner of speech.

Rereading these poems, published in 1982 but out of print for over a decade, I have been moved again by their razor sharp honesty. They have brought in their wake a cascade of images, a specific iconography, that sweeps me back to the enormous, thronged, madcap Kālī temple in Calcutta that gave the modern city its name. It hardly matters that Rāmprasād considered priestly ritual, worship of statues, animal slaughter, recitation of prayers, or the lighting of lamps, to be largely devoid of merit. The temple at Kalikatha is something! It could be an architecture built from his poems.

Should you ever get to Calcutta, go search out the

temple some evening, in the south part of the city away from the noise and industrial soot of downtown. With its surrounding maze of boisterous colorful shops, trinket stalls, kitchens, brassy shrines, fortune tellers, beggars, lepers, energetic hucksters, and priests, the Kālī temple is a great microcosm of life and a steady destination for pilgrims. Here the earth, where a severed finger of the Great Mother once fell, is chewed by thousands of feet, hoofs, and automobile tires. It is a vast cauldron of mud and spittle, cook oil and motor oil, dust, food, shit, bright scarlet flower petals and spattered blood that's a bit darker. Lines of busses and taxis idle their motors by the front entrance. Yet it makes a compelling refuge from present-day Calcutta. Somehow the crowds and confusion make sense when you draw near the Goddess.

The temple has a viewing platform where you go, if you haven't fasted and purified yourself the requisite number of days, to take *darshan* (spiritual viewing) with the precious long-tongued Kālī image. In 1993 an official sign hung above:

> It is Forbidden
> to deceive Pilgrims
> while Ceremonies
> are in Progress

Facing that sign is like facing Rāmprasād's poetry. It forces the mind toward a paradox you can't ever escape. Don't think you can get through this world without losing everything! Don't imagine the Goddess plays by your rules! The single most compelling quality of Rāmprasād Sen is how he recklessly confronts the endless round of deceptions—deceptions by others, of oneself by oneself, of even the most earnest seeker by the Mother who spins out her web of Māyā.

Orthodox Hindus have generally looked on Goddess cults with a mixture of condescension and distaste. In anthropological terms you could say it's the dominant culture's anxiety around native people who still follow old telluric ways. More directly, it's got to do with the mutability and chaos of the feminine itself, which anyone finds if not scary at least pretty baffling. Here's a ninth-century poem by the amiable Bengali poet, Yogeshvara, a sort of ethnographic snapshot of India's indigenous culture.

> The tribesmen dispatch
> creature after
> living creature to Durgā,
> Goddess who dwells in a craggy wilderness grotto.
> They slosh the blood on a field-spirit tree.
> Then joined by their women at dusk
> go wild to the gourd-lute
> stopping just to pass liquor around—
> the old way—
> in a bilva fruit husk.

This kind of Earth Goddess orgy, no doubt familiar to Rāmprasād, still takes place. I have seen in the hills of Bihar and Orissa the little shrines in the groves, with their well-trampled dance-ground, the sacrifice-posts, the spirit trees wrapped in gay cloth. Clay pots hang in the palm trees to catch sap for the liquor. But please do not rush off to see these things! It was the genius of Rāmprasād's poetry to lift the old tribal practices and in a cosmopolitan and psychologically astute manner intertwine them with the *tantrika's* belief that we animate an inner spiritual landscape. The secret of his poetry is that worship of the Goddess is a powerful personal drama—a devotional yoga—in which the creatures sacrificed are one's own fondest delusions. In which the celebratory dance-ground is one's own liberated mind.

The evidence suggests that Rāmprasād sung his poems and never made books. The people who first wrote them down treated the manuscripts as spiritually potent objects. In 1853 a Bengali poet, Isvarachandra Gupta, described his decades-long search for copies of Rāmprasād poems.

> Works of his which had been collected together earlier have by now almost disappeared, because in those days people used to guard them carefully like some secret mantra, not showing them to anyone even at the cost of their lives, bringing them out only at puja time to decorate with flowers and sandalwood paste, as some people still do today, and though we would have given all we had we were not able to obtain any of the verses. Hidden in this way they have become completely destroyed. Worms and other insects ate them, moisture decomposed them, fire burned them, they were used by the impotent as charms to secure beautiful women or long life....
>
> (translated by Malcolm McLean)

For good or for ill, things that for centuries were hidden away, or remained the possession of a particular people, are now out where anyone with a little effort and the price of a book can find them. This is true of Rāmprasād's *tantric* poetry, which you could say was hidden on the streets of Bengal in the mouths of largely nonliterate singers for so many decades. Now those poems come out and speak with refreshing honesty to the human condition. We Americans are privileged to see them.

I believe there are reasons certain teachings do not get handed out indiscriminately. Why some old poetries are jealously guarded. Perhaps it's unwise to talk in too loud a voice of Kālī's odd habits—the fierce drunkenness, the charnel ground howling, the sexy barebreasted dance on a corpse. Maybe such talk should wait till the children have gone off to bed. That's the time to pull Rāmprasād Sen's poetry off the shelf and see what it holds. The teachings are difficult, but they might set you free.

PREFACE
to the Second Edition

It would seem to be, indeed, an auspicious moment to republish our particular selection of Rāmprasād's lyrics in English translation, for this incarnation of *Grace and Mercy* is supported by and surrounded with offerings from two other authors. Preceding the republication of our book by little more than a year came Malcolm McLean's study of Rāmprasād entitled *Devoted to the Goddess: The Life and Work of Rāmprasād* (Albany, N.Y.: State University of New York Press, 1998). Following, or possibly appearing about the same time as ours, will be two works from a single author, Rachel Fell McDermott. One of them, entitled *Mother of My Heart, Daughter of My Dreams: The Transformations of Kali and Uma in the Devotional Poetry of Bengal* (N.Y. and London: Oxford University Press, in press), is a history of Bengali Shakta poets and their songs, beginning with Rāmprasād (ca. 1718-1775) and extending through the stellar and prolific Kazi Nazrul Islam (1899-1976) and beyond, right up to the present. The other work is a substantial collection of Shakta poetry by diverse poets, translated by McDermott, *Singing to the Goddess: Poems to Kali and Uma from Bengal* (N.Y. and London: Oxford University Press, in press). Rāmprasād will be featured prominently in this latter anthology, for Rāmprasād occupies uncontested within the tradition itself the position of both the first and still the greatest of the Bengali Shakta lyricists.

McLean's study should be of interest to the readers of *Grace and Mercy* for several reasons. He includes a number of translations, some partial, some whole, of Rāmprasād's poetry. Moreover, McLean calls to our attention, employing a Foucauldian approach to authorship, that the Bengali-speaking community is in a certain sense as much an author of the corpus of Rāmprasād's poetry as is Rāmprasād himself. For, it is the appreciative community who might have kept Rāmprasād's poetry alive orally, or who might have jotted down lyrics heard, or who might even have edited what it both heard and committed to writing. The community, anonymous and made up of many self-appointed editors, is the vehicle by which Rāmprasād's lyrics—those lyrics attributed to Rāmprasād, anyway—have come down to us. Those lyrics were printed for limited public scrutiny for the first time only in the middle of the nineteenth century, well after Rāmprasād's death. And, suggests McLean, those self-appointed editors anywhere along the way and at any time may also have been self-appointed censors of sorts. They may also have been self-appointed co-poets, inserting into Rāmprasād's corpus a line or two, or an entire lyric, of their own making. What we think of as Rāmprasād's poetry is probably that but possibly a bit more, or a bit less. And we readers should be aware of that possibility.

A second point McLean argues in his book should also be kept in mind as one reads through the poems in *Grace and Mercy* or any collection of Rāmprasād's poetry. McLean is convinced that Rāmprasād was more thoroughly a *tantrik* than the tradition has made him out to be and that all of Rāmprasād's lyrics perforce must be read as *tantrik* statements. And here is where McDermott's *Mother of My Heart, Daughter of My Dreams* puts McLean's point into some perspective. McDermott documents well and convincingly that the history of the Shakta lyric in Bengali is a history of the "sweetening" of Shakta lyrics from the time of Rāmprasād to the present. By "sweetening" she means a transformation from the more *tantrik* to the more "devotional," represented by the term *bhakti*. *Bhakti* implies an emotional relationship of the devotee with his or her chosen deity. *Bhakti*, in Bengal, had been before the time of Rāmprasād and is still today in large part associated with Vaishnava religious expression, where Krishṇa is the primary deity. Clearly Vaishnava *bhakti* has left its mark on Shakta poetry, but when does this come about? Was Rāmprasād so influenced? Does his poetry reflect infusions of devotional *bhakti*, of a Vaishnava *dvaita* or dualistic perception of separation of devotee (the devotee's soul) from the deity? McLean, being a strict constructionist of the *tantrik* Rāmprasād, says no for Rāmprasād's poetry. Consequently, when Rāmprasād sings "Sugar I love / But haven't the slightest desire / To merge with sugar" (54), one of his most famous lyrics, McLean is at pains to try to explain away this seeming dualistic sentiment. In the end, he simply declares Rāmprasād's statement to be *tantrik* and invokes the name of Ramakrishna, the nineteenth-century saintly Shakta who, McLean avers, understood these lines of poetry in the same manner as McLean himself does. Despite McLean's efforts to keep Rāmprasād purely *tantrik*, McDermott's "sweetening" seems clearly at work here. One could, of course, put the blame for this sugaring upon one of those anonymous self-appointed redactors, if one feels the need to do so.

We concluded our introduction to the first edition of *Grace and Mercy In Her Wild Hair* by calling our readers' attention to two works of translated poetry similar in some respects to that of Rāmprasād's, similar in that they were collections of religious poetry as poetic as they were religious. We would like to end these introductory remarks by mentioning yet another work in that genre, Andrew Schelling, translator, *For Love of the Dark One: Songs of Mirabai* (1998), published by this same Hohm Press.

PREFACE AND ACKNOWLEDGMENTS
to the First Edition

Any translator of the extraordinary Bengali devotional poet, Rāmprasād Sen, has to deal with two depressingly persistent problems: first, the variation of texts for single poems, a condition partly explained by the dependence of recorders and editors on the oral tradition of transmitting verses meant to be sung; second, questionable authorship. Many of the poems assigned to Rāmprasād are probably the work of other (not always bad) poets affixing the greater writer's name to their own work, perhaps to help it on the way to glory. No serious scholarly effort has yet been made to establish a settled canon, a task that in any case may prove futile. The authors have received helpful advice in generous portions from the following among their colleagues and friends: Edward C. Dimock, Jr., Ralph W. Nicholas, A.K. Ramanujan, Tirthankar Bose, Pabitra Sarkar, William Brandt, Kenneth Bryant, John Gage, Robert Goldman, Josephine Miles, Vinayak Paranjpe, and Thomas Sloane.

To these all we wish to express our deep gratitude and to absolve them from responsibility for any of the errors in this book; these, of course, rest with us. Wallace Stevens wrote that the "moon follows the sun like a French/ Translation of a Russian poem." We hope that here and there we have reflected so much of the original light.

INTRODUCTION

I. Background

The poems of Rāmprasād Sen emerge from the con-
text of a very old Indian religious cult, one with which
orthodox Hindus sometimes find themselves uncomfort-
able. Whether they were first composed orally or written
down, the poems were meant to be sung and for an audi-
ence of villagers whose expectations rose out of a life
that changed little over the centuries. When all this is ad-
mitted, one has to concede that the word "translation" is,
at best, a dubious one for what follows: literary verses by
contemporary western city dwellers. Yet the translators
thought that something of the power and sense of
Rāmprasād's work might be brought over into the mod-
ern American idiom if we used a style comparable to the
"openness" and colloquialism of the originals.

Our method was simple and one used many times
before, particularly with Indian poetry. A specialist in the
original and one or more poets in the receiving language
work together through various stages: a deliberately pro-
saic translation with notes, a verse translation, criticism
of this, revisions, until the participants are satisfied—the
specialist that the English version strays from the origi-
nal as little as possible, the poet that the final draft is a

poem. The method is open to obvious criticisms—chiefly, that the poet, no matter how good the specialist, must work from an interpretation of the original and thereby compounds the possibility of misrepresentation. This criticism is legitimate and there is no point dodging it. But until there are more American poets who are also specialists in languages like Bengali, the method seems the only one that might produce something worth reading, if the aim is to make poems in the receiving language. Though prose versions can serve good purposes, it was our thought that, no matter how culturally exotic Rāmprasād Sen seems to late twentieth-century Americans, we may still read his work as poetry. In fact, he shares two decisive qualities with our contemporary poets: an intense feeling for the desperateness of the human condition, and a conviction that the poet's personality is a proper subject matter for his poems.

But though Rāmprasād is not shy about letting his personal feelings into his songs and these songs are still part of a living oral tradition, we know almost nothing about his life except that he was born and flourished in the Bengal of the eighteenth century.[1] Our ignorance is not surprising. The lives of pre-modern Indian poets were often transmuted into exemplary types of what they should have been. Rāmprasād in this fashion became the ideal type of devotional poet. Legend has it that, as a young clerk bored with his work and suffused with devotion, he was caught filling his ledger with songs to the Mother Goddess and was sent off, adequately subsidized, by his kindly employer to devote his whole time to worship. Even his death exemplified a perfect act of worship. At the climax of the festival for the Goddess whom he adored, Her image is immersed in the Ganges. The poet is said to have followed Her under, singing lyrics he composed to elicit Her grace. And so closed his life, in its ideal telling, of perfect faith.

About that faith we know a good deal more than we do about Rāmprasād Sen. It was a species of *bhakti*. The term *bhakti*, signifying emotional worship, is found as far back as the Upanishads.[2] But it takes on its special meaning as defining a religious movement during what is called the medieval period in India. *Bhakti* is the term describing a group of cults that shared then at least two things in common: the spirit of revolt against brahman-dominated Hindu orthodoxy, and the aim of achieving a direct passionate relation with a particular deity that orthodoxy prevented.[3] The orthodox faith entailed intercession between believer and god. The intercessor was the brahman priest who commanded the appropriate ritual knowledge to achieve contact with divine power. But too often the priest was merely a technician of the ceremonial, and the ritual a routine that did not much satisfy those who longed for something more personal and intense, more "real." This was precisely, in its various forms, what *bhakti* supplied. For the priest, it substituted the guru who did not intercede but guided, and the guidance was toward immediate relation with the divine, either in mystic union or loving closeness. Like the orthodox faith, *bhakti* was a means of release from the racking world of rebirth and the chain of cause and effect, of karma—not, however through arid ritual, but through a wholly devoted heart.

The dominant modes of *bhakti* were those connected with the worship of Vishṇu, either in the form of the heroic Rāma or the lovable Krishṇa, and of Shiva, often in His most terrifying aspects. Rāmprasād's *bhakti* was none of these, but worship of Shiva's consort, Shakti, the Great Mother. And though Shaktism was never so prevalent a cult in India as Vaishnavism and Shaivism, it commanded a wide following in Bengal, sharing dominance there with Krishṇa cults and the Muslim faith.

How does Shaktism differ from the other *bhakti* cults? A major difference, obviously, is the worship of a goddess as the prime divinity. The worship of a female principle, if nothing else, permits a range and intensity of relationship to deity not readily available to other forms of *bhakti*. That Rāmprasād responds to the Goddess in various aspects with various names, and by no means exhaustively, suggests the rich range of emotional expressiveness She opens to Her devotees.

But does his response suggest more? And what sense is there to be made out of the fact that some of Her forms and titles seem flatly to contradict others and that they all add up to no clear and coherent definition of Her character? For example, some epithets for Her denote a loving mother or lovable child, while others indicate an overwhelming destructive force. Some point to a transcendental deity, Shiva, forbidding denizen of mountaintop and cremation grounds. Thus, while She is addressed as the Mother (and most often perceived in that role by Rāmprasād), She is also known as Kālī, the Dark One, of terrible and menacing aspect. She is sometimes Umā, daughter of the Mountain (Giri), who as a tender girl is married to the unprepossessing Shiva; at other times She is Durgā, fair complexioned protectress, who, mounted on Her lion, slays the buffalo demon, Mahishāsura, who is released from rebirth by Her very touch. Though conceived as a warrior, She is most often seen as motherly, both to Her divine children (Her sons are Gaṇesh and Kārtik, Her daughters, Lakshmī and Sarasvatī) and to Her devotees. She presides over men's happier experiences: prosperity, victory and good luck. But She has many more names besides these—108 is one figure—including many that designate Her role as the female counterpart of Shiva. Thus, as He is given the epithet Bhairava (the Terrible One), so She is Bhairavī. And so on—a vast collection of titles that seem to add up to no whole, no consistent ethos. But this confusion holds only if She is seen as human. Seen as a principle, She deserves Her many names. For while it is perhaps true that these epithets indicate that more than one female deity has been absorbed into Her character and that some of the epithets may be ways of explaining otherwise puzzling cult iconography or ritual, Her names, together, do finally describe what She is— the vital principle of the visible universe which has many faces: gracious, cruel, creative, destructive, loving, indifferent—the endless possibility of the active energy at the heart of the world. If devotees sometimes call her Kālī, sometimes Tārā, it is not because they are confused or that She is a chaos of attributes, but because they are addressing the aspect of Her that in the particular circumstances they wish to bring into their consciousness, or they are using one name as a sort of metonymy for all the others.

In Rāmprasād's songs we meet many of Her faces
and necessarily become involved in the context of Her
mythical biography. For example, we see Her sometimes
as the child Gaurī, sometimes as the young Umā or Pārvatī,
the devoted bride of Shiva, who had for a rival the River
Ganges, Shiva's second wife, whom He caught in His
hair as She fell from heaven. But more often we face the
Goddess in a less benign form, particularly where She
has assimilated many of the characteristics of Her ascetic
husband, one of whose epithets is Kāla (meaning both
death and time), the masculine counterpart for the name
so often used for Her.[4] She is represented as blue-black,
three-eyed, four-armed, naked except for the macabre
adornment of a necklace of human heads and a girdle of
lopped-off hands. Like Shiva as the Lord of Dancers, She
is portrayed in the midst of a great dance, hair flying, Her
whole being in ecstatic trance.[5] However, this dance in-
cludes elements special to the Goddess. Hers is clearly a
battle dance, as can be seen from the lethal blade She
wields. Her platform is the inert body of Shiva. Other
representations—for example of a single deity, half male,
half female—suggest that, to Her devotees, there is no
single simple way of perceiving the mystery of reality, at
least not in human terms. The sum of all Her representa-
tions, however, points to an overwhelming paradox com-
manding awed worship beyond conventional religious
usage, just as Kālī and Her husband stand outside the so-
cial order in their behavior and habitat. *Bhakti*, as we have
noted, began as a defiance of orthodoxy. It is hardly any
wonder that its deities thrived outside of the comfortable
confines of established belief.

Rāmprasād accepts this unorthodoxy as the true way of salvation and in his songs draws heavily on other unorthodox sources, chiefly the very old esoteric doctrines of Tantra and Yoga, both by this time related to the worship of the Great Mother in cults deeply rooted in Bengal. In these doctrines the way to release is not in passionate prayer alone, in songs like those of Rāmprasād, where the Goddess is perceived as external to the *bhakta*. In Tantra, She is rather conceived as an internal principle, part of the allegorized physio-religious landscape of the body, a vital force, which proper discipline will bring into relation with Her devotee's higher self. Thus, the spinal column is perceived as a sort of plant with seven lotuses on its stem; the first of these is called the *mulādhāra cakra* and is located between the anus and the genitalia. The others, each with its name, ascend to the highest, the *sahasrāra* or thousand-petalled lotus located in the center of the crown of the head. Each petal of each lotus has also its distinctive name. The dormant Shakti is said to reside, in the form of *kulakuṇḍalinī*, at the lowest of the *cakras* and through proper means is to be brought, stage by stage, up the channels—there are three running parallel to the spinal chord—until She enters the *sahasrāra* where yoga (union) with Shiva takes place.[6] The representation of the Goddess standing on Shiva's chest is a metaphor for this union.[7] The whole allegory of the union provides other metaphors for Rāmprasād's poems, for example, poem 46, in which the devotee is urged to dive into his own body and bring up the *kulakuṇḍalinī* that is here depicted as a great pearl in the sea of knowledge.

In fact, much that on first glance seems obscure in

Rāmprasād becomes clear if seen as part of this great inner drama of salvation that characterizes Shaktism: for instance, his scorn for caste, ritual, idol worship, pilgrimage, animal sacrifice—all externals in which he finds no religious content, and which are in fact obstacles in attaining release from the world. What he does find of value, besides the words of his guru, is his own fervent devotion, that inward state in which all energies are concentrated on the great striving toward the divine. Only his passionate concentration will get him across the sea of life. Only total devotion will protect him from his worst enemies, the six passions—sexual desire, anger, greed, lethargy, pride and envy—which appear in the poems in many guises: crocodiles, thieves, villains, tenants in his body's house, oil merchants, oxen. But whatever form they take, their sole function is to cheat him of release from the cycle of rebirth. They work hand in hand with Māyā or appearance (which ironically is the work of the Goddess Herself in Her role as creator) to cut Rāmprasād off from the reality toward which he struggles. His songs are in fact continual reminders to himself of this truth as well as prayers to the Mother that She might effect his release by the favor of Her grace.

II. The Poetry

I'm not calling you Mother anymore.
All you give me is trouble.
I had a home and a family, now
I'm a beggar—what will You think of
Next, my wild-haired Devī?

I'll beg before I come to You,
Crying "Mother." I've tried that
And got the silent treatment.
If the mother lives should the son suffer,
And if she's dead, hasn't he got to live somehow?

Rāmprasād says: What's a mother
Anyway, the son's worst enemy?
I keep wondering what worse You can do
Than make me live over and over
The pain, life after life.   [24]

This is typical Rāmprasād: a petulant outburst, as if the poem had begun in passionate mid-quarrel; this followed by a bitter itemization of the poet's misery; this, in turn, capped by the poet's signature affixed, as it were, to a bill of complaints against the Goddess, and finally a general statement of the tortured relation between devotee and deity. The aim in such poetry is to make its audience live with the poet the actual condition of the devotee moving through the experiences that will lead eventually to release from the hateful cycle of rebirth. Rāmprasād's method is to get in as close as possible to the actual relation between the poet, tangled in the snares of the world, and the object of his worship, remote in the condition of total freedom. He accomplishes this by foregrounding, on the one hand, the poet's unidealized human condition and on the other, balancing that off with the view—from the human vantage—of the character of the Goddess. This view, full of rage and irony, might seem to Westerners a piece of near blasphemous irreverence, but is, in fact, a convention found in other Indian devotional verse.[8]

Rāmprasād is one of its most frequent and daring practitioners, and it serves him in many ways. Its precatory function is to get the attention of the deity, the psychological principle evidently being that insult is more apt to provoke response from a self-absorbed deity than a mere summons or even flattery. But the device has more complex poetic functions. It is a way of dramatizing the difficult and ambiguous relation of devotee and deity in a world that is built, so to speak, to keep the human and the divine spirit apart, and it suggests the painful exertion involved in the posture of worship. But the convention is also a means of revealing the power in that relation, once established, to transform every kind of emotion—hostile as well as loving—into devotional passion through the act of total concentration on the deity. Finally, the device serves as an ironic instrument to exhibit what is essential in the relations between devotee and deity. For when Rāmprasād accuses Kālī of indifference, he is also suggesting her total detachment from the world, the very quality that he needs to achieve for release, just as when he accuses her of shameless nakedness, intoxication, and madness, he is, in fact, cataloging some of her most potent attributes: the awesome presence of real being, without the conventional covering of appearance; the joy of true freedom, and its refusal to be contained in rational or moral categories. And when he bemoans his own misery and his unattended need for his mother, he is marking the essential starting point for the worshipper who has begun to see his true relation with the world. Here, the devotee's anguish measures the distance between human and divine, just as poems that exhibit joy suggest the closing of that distance. The convention of accusation and insult, in short, provides Rāmprasād with an intensity and depth of feeling to match the awesome crisis of salvation.

Yet Rāmprasād's use of this convention is not even his most startling practice, if seen against the background of Indian classical tradition. More drastic is the introduction of the poet's personality into his poems. The Sanskrit poet of the older tradition, typically, stayed well behind his verse, entering it, if at all, in the character of an ideal type, just as his characters and situations were ideal.[9] The personal, with rare exceptions, he would have regarded as sub-literary.[10] But it was not the poet of the classical tradition that served Rāmprasād for a model in his devotional songs, but rather the passionate worshipper, the *bhakta*, speaking in his own voice directly to the issue of his salvation. If most medieval devotional or *bhakti* poetry aimed to arouse a sense of loving closeness to the deity, then Rāmprasād's particular style of *bhakti* carried him a step further—to using his own life as a poetic exhibit of striving for that closeness. And the intensity of his personalism makes him stand out even among other *bhakti* poets whose expressive range was, in fact, formidable.

The poetry associated with the devotional movements was mainly of three kinds: the hortatory, in which the poet—really a guru—who had attained understanding, instructed an audience that still needed to be shown the way; the dramatic, in which the poet identified with lover, friend, or kinsman of the deity as a person in a particular phase of its activity of play;[11] and finally, the lyric in which the deity appears as a person. It is mainly this latter kind of poem that represents a break with the classical Sanskrit tradition; the other two fall well within the range of the tradition of the impersonal poem.

Yet there is an exception to this last generalization. *Bhakti* poetry, and Rāmprasād's is no exception, almost always ends with a signature line or *bhaṇitā* in which the poet, interjecting the personal in a manner appropriate to the *bhakti* mode, may speak in his own voice. However, even this introduction of the personal could become highly formulaic with usage. Rāmprasād uses the *bhaṇitā* for a number of conventional purposes: sometimes as a summary statement of stance, sometimes as an ironic commentary on the body of the poem. The device, in its most basic function, probably serves him and all its users as a refrain joining the songs of a cycle for oral presentation.[12]

Rāmprasād composed in all three of the above-mentioned modes, occasionally taking on the role of lecturer (52),[13] sometimes speaking in the voice of the mother of Umā, the Mountain's divine child whose husband will be that weird and unprepossessing mendicant, Shiva (33).[14] Sometimes Rāmprasād even mixes the modes (61), but his imagination seems most engaged by the third in which he speaks for himself, though even here, the model or metaphor for the relation between him and the Goddess is familiar, that of son to mother, as in the poem that opened this discussion. He is also fond of translating the hortatory mode into something characteristically personal as when, in many poems, he substitutes for the audience that requires enlightenment, his own mind:

Who's with you Mind,
And what are you waiting for?   [12][15]

So I say: Mind, don't you sleep
Or Time is going to get in and steal from you.[13]

Mind, why do you fret so much,
Like a motherless child?   [45]

    The ostensible audience here, the poet's mind, is not
at all depersonalized as with the usual hortatory poem,
but as is so characteristic in Rāmprasād's work, made part
of the family, a sort of easily fooled, reckless younger
brother needing stern, frequent, but loving correction.
Indeed, Rāmprasād peoples his verse with personifica-
tions which in lesser poets might remain vaguely abstract,
but in his work become vivid actors in the drama of his
experience. His passions and senses rise up as physically
present antagonists, along with death, a less than intimate
but no less real opponent in Rāmprasād's battle for re-
lease.
    Even to the worn conventions of traditional Sanskrit
verse Rāmprasād restores life by setting them deep in the
experiential quality of his version of *bhakti*. Old figures
of traditional allegory—for instance, boat and house as
metaphors for the body, net for delusion, jewel for wis-
dom, and sea for both the world of appearance and for the
waters of salvation—all these become palpable things in
his work, part of the setting of his struggle for salvation,
and here they thrive in a rich climate of feeling ranging
from the wild despair of an abandoned child (17) through

the intoxicated hilarity of a man drunk with Kālī's saving love (59) to something like the high calm of a worshipper tasting release (51).

Rāmprasād has no visible predecessors in his extraordinary versions of *bhakti*.[16] The complex intensity of his relation with his deity is hardly matched in any other poet. Other poets have brilliantly exploited the material he uses, but none in his extraordinary combination that altogether produces a unique voice in Indian literature. Some modern readers, viewing the perfect end of devotion as oneness with God, may sometimes find the tone of that voice hard to take undiluted; Rāmprasād can coolly inform us that, though he loves sugar, he hasn't "the slightest desire/ To merge with sugar" (54), and who with awesome honesty tells Kālī to Her face that nobody would worship Her if it weren't for the terror of death (4), and with equally disarming candor and considerable self-irony, concludes a poem with the following admission:

> It's amazing!
> Others brag about their happiness,
> I brag about my suffering.   [28]

It might even occur to the reader that Rāmprasād seems on occasion to contradict himself about the desired end of salvation, for at one point he declares that what he wants of the Goddess is not union, but proximity: "...what's this salvation / If it swallows the saved like water / In water?" (54). But at another point he can say: "...you end, brother, / Where you begin, a reflection / Rising in water, mixing with water, / Finally one with water" (3). In this last, he may be speaking only about the body, but clearly he seems to be influenced by the dualistic view (*dvaita*) of Krishṇa cults, as against the monistic Hinduism (*advaita*) common to Shiva and Shakti worship. But most readers aren't theologians and can take Rāmprasād for what he is: a poet of great gifts singing out of a dreadful urgency in a voice that is full and memorably human. It is no wonder that his verses are still sung by the old and young in Bengali villages and towns.

In Bengal, Rāmprasād is appreciated as much for the music he brought to his words as for the poetry itself. That aural delicacy, of course, is missed completely when one comes to these lyrics through translations. In some of the published Bengali anthologies, a melody or melodic style and rhythm are specified for each of the songs. In some cases a particular *rāgiṇī*, a given scale or mode, is indicated. But for the majority, the designated music is simply "*prāsadī*," an adjectival form of Rāmprasād's name, which underscores the uniqueness of this poet's music. The prosody of these songs is governed more by the specified musical rhythmic configuration (most frequently *ektālā*, a twelve-beat measure) than by any of the traditional poetic scansion systems. Several syllables may be rushed together or a single syllable lengthened to meet the demands of oral performance. But the songs do display that most common of poetic ornamentations—common to medieval Bengali poetry, at least—the end-rhyme. It is partly with end-rhymes and the musical rhythmic pattern that one kind of artistic unity is obtained. Another unity, the poetic unity inherent in these texts *sans* music and rhyme, comes through, we trust, in our translations.

Interested readers may want to enjoy the English renderings of some sixteenth- and seventeenth-century Vaishṇava devotional poetry from Bengal as well as a sampling of tenth- to twelve-century Shaiva lyrics originally composed in the Kannada language. The first are to be found in *In Praise of Krishna: Songs from the Bengali*, Edward C. Dimock, Jr. and Denise Levertov, trans. (Garden City, N.Y.: Anchor Books, 1967), the second in *Speaking of Siva*, A. K. Ramanajan, trans. (Baltimore: Penguin Books Inc., 1973).

NOTES TO INTRODUCTION

1. Direct information about Rāmprasād is almost nonexistent and is compromised by doubt. We have details about the poet as reported by Isvar Chandra Gupta in his magazine, *Saṁbād Prabhākar*. But these belong to the nineteenth century and constitute shaky testimony. Discussion in English of Rāmprasād's biography is found in Romesh Chunder Dutt, *Cultural Heritage of Bengal*, 3rd ed. rev. (Calcutta: Punthi Pustak, 1962), pp. 79 ff.; and Sukumar Sen, *History of Bengali Literature* (New Delhi: Sahitya Akademi, 1960), pp. 169-70. In Bengali, see Isvar Chandra Gupta's article reprinted in Yogendranath Gupta, *Sādhak Kabi Rāmprasād* (Calcutta: Bhattacharya Sons, Ltd., 1954) pp. 6 ff.; and Sukumar Sen, *Bāṇgālā Sāhityer Itihās*, vol. 1, pt. 2, 2nd ed. (Calcutta: Eastern Publishers, 1965), pp. 493 ff.

2. The *Shvetāshvatara Upanishad* (see S. K. De, "Sects and Sectarian Worship in the Epic," *Aspects of Sanskrit Literature* [Calcutta: K. L. Mukhopadhyay, 1959] pp. 57 ff.). *Bhakti* is one traditional Hindu means of salvation (*moksha* or release from rebirth)

along with *jñāna* (knowledge of the reality behind appearances, come to through contemplation and study). But *bhakti*, in the form of organized cults, did not come to prominence until fairly late in Indian history. (See Edward C. Dimock, Jr., "Hindu Mysticism," *Encyclopaedia Britannica*, 15th ed. [Chicago: Encyclopaedia Britannica, 1974], vol. 8, pp. 923 ff.)

3. See A. K. Ramanujan, *Speaking of Siva*, pp. 29-37.

4. Though *Kāla* is one of the many epithets for Shiva, the name more commonly used in Bengali for this god is Mahākāla (The Great Time or Death). In these lyrics "Death" (*kāla*) usually refers to Yama, not Shiva. Mention should be made of another name for Shiva, the Blue-Throated One, an epithet acquired when, in order to save the world, he drank the poison churned up from the cosmic sea (38).

5. See Ananda K. Coomaraswamy, *The Dance of Shiva* (New York: The Sunwise Turn, Inc., 1918), pp. 66-78, for a detailed discussion of the significance of Shiva's dance. It should be noted that the *naṭarāja* aspect of Shiva does not appear in Rāmprasād's Shaktism. In his lyrics Shiva is the two-armed, white-skinned *yogī*, husband of Kālī.

6. Jadunath Sinha, *Rama Prasada's Devotional Songs*, "Introduction," pp. 29-32.

7. Shiva is the *purusha*, the inactive; the Goddess is the *shakti* or *prakriti*, the active. Without His shakti (power) Shiva is powerless. Until yoga (union) occurs, Shiva is like a *shava* (corpse). (See Heinrich Zimmer, *Myths and Symbols in Indian Art and Civilization* [New York: Pantheon Books, 1946], pp. 205-16.)

8. The convention seems to have no technical name, though certain figures in Sanskrit poetics vaguely resemble it, like *nindāstuti* (praise by blame), *vyājastuti* (pretext of praise), and *vyājaninda* (pretext of blame). However, these are used mainly as witty compliment or insult, as when a king is "censured" for his cruelty in making widows of his enemy's wives. *Bhakti* poets aimed at something far less courtly in their usage. It is possible that Rāmprasād adapted for his own uses the censure of Shiva from the Purāṇic tradition, in which Daksha, Brahmā's son, in a fit of pique, denounces Shiva for many of the faults that Rāmprasād attributed to Kālī and Shiva: immod-

esty, slovenliness, evil companions, hysteria, morbid obsession with death, drunkenness and insanity (see, for example, the *Bhagavata Purāṇa: The Srimad-Bhagavatam of Krishna-Dwaipayana Vyasa*, J. M. Sanyal, tr. [Calcutta: Oriental Pub. Co., 1952, 3rd ed.], vol. 11, ch. 2, pp. 8-11). It is not a great step for a *bhakti* poet to transpose the speaker of these denunciations from the third person to the first and use them to very different ends. Another source of the convention could be folk traditions like the slanging contest from whose ribaldry even gods were not spared.

9. Even when the Sanskrit author alludes to himself in his work, the intention is understood by the audience to be tactical, very much in the manner of Pindar in his odes, where the point is often to establish the poet's credentials as a spokesman whose voice properly transcends the personal. (See Elroy L. Bundy, *Studia Pindarica II, The First Isthmain Ode*, No 2. [Berkeley: University of California Press, 1962], pp.35-92; also *Studia Pindarica I, The Eleventh Olympian Ode*, [Berkeley: University of California Press, 1962] pp. 1-34, especially p. 32.)

10. There are, of course, exceptions stretching as far back as the *Rig Veda*, for example, the well-known "Gambler's Hymn" (34, Bk. 10), also Hymn 164, Bk. 1, in which there is a vivid sense of the poet. In these the emphasis is placed somewhat more than usual on the condition of the supplicant, whereas the typical hymn was almost wholly given over to a catalogue of the attributes and accomplishments of the deity addressed. And this latter mode is the overwhelmingly dominant one for the later Indian hymn or *stotra*, until at least the medieval period. (See De, "Sanskrit Devotional Poetry and Hymnology," *Aspects of Sanskrit Literature*, pp. 101 ff.)

11. Many of Kabir's poems illustrate the hortatory kind; examples of the second are most typically found in poems on the play of the young Krishṇa in which the poet takes on the role of foster parent or his beloved Radha or the "friend" bearing messages between god and lover. Sur Das is celebrated for poems in which the speaker identifies with the parent; Chandidās, for those in which the speaker takes the role of lover or friend. (See E. C. Dimock and D. Levertov, *In Praise of Krishna*.)

12. The signature line has sometimes been omitted in other translations of *bhakti* verse. This has not been our practice, which was based on the assumption that when the poet included a *bhaṇitā*, he did so for a purpose vital to his poem.

13. Though, as usual for him, with considerable irony.

14. This kind of poem is based upon a number of Indian commonplaces, for example, that of the mother resisting giving away her child-daughter in marriage, particularly to a husband with Shiva's appalling credentials. There are strong hints of this commonplace at work in the fifth and eighth cantos of Kālidāsa's *Kumāra-sambhava*, where it is clear that Umā's mother is hardly happy either with her daughter's service to or marriage with Shiva.

15. The apostrophe to one's own mind is also a convention of Indian religious verse.

16. But he has some followers of more or less talent (see Thompson and Spencer, *Bengali Religious Lyrics, Sakta*).

The Poems

1

I spent my days in fun,
Now, Time's up and I'm out of a job.
I used to go here and there making money,
Had brothers, friends, wife, and children
Who listened when I spoke. Now they scream at me
Just because I'm poor. Death's
Field man is going to sit by my pillow
Waiting to grab my hair, and my friends
And relations will stack up the bier,
Fill the pitcher, ready my shroud and say
So long to the old boy
In his holy man's get-up.
They'll shout Hari a few times,
Dump me on the pile and walk off.
That's it for old Rāmprasād.
They'll wipe off the tears
And dig in to their supper.

2

O Mind, you think it's all in fun,
You've got it made, really made,
Bouncing from mood to mood,
Bawling now, now dancing.
When there was money you spent a fortune
On trash. When there was none,
You sold jewels for next to nothing.

Beauty lives in the pleasure house
And you are dazzled by Beauty.
When are you going to wake up
And count the cost of Beauty?

3

*T*ell me, brother, what happens after death?
The whole world is arguing about it—
Some say you become a ghost,
Others that you go to heaven,
And some that you get close to God,
And the Vedas insist you're a bit of sky
Reflected in a jar fated to shatter.

When you look for sin and virtue in nothing,
You end up with nothing.
The elements live in the body together
But go their own ways at death.

Prasād says: you end, brother,
Where you began, a reflection
Rising in water, mixing with water,
Finally one with water.

4

Pitying Mother, do I worshipYou
Out of my own free will?
Nobody would
If it weren't for the terror
Of death.

Where are You, then, Mother,
Whose strength was before
All other powers? Your name
Is the only freedom.

O Devī of the tripled gaze,
Who else has that strength?

5

$\mathscr{T}$he fisherman has cast his net
And sits there waiting, waiting.

What will become of me,
Mother, in this world?

The fish are safest
In deep waters.

The fisherman has cast this world
As his net.

When he sees what he wants
He grabs it by the hair.

There's no way out, so, Mind,
What will you do, bound by Death?

Rāmprasād says: Call the Mother,
She can handle Death.

6

Listen to this story, Mother Tārā,
My house is a battlefield, nothing but a quarrel
Of cross purposes, Five Senses,
Mother, each with a different desire,
All wanting pleasure all the time.

I have been born in eight million forms
And now I'm born a man,
A funny figure in a world
Whose gift to us is a load of misery.

Mother, look at Rāmprasād
Trying to live in this house
Whose master is driven crazy,
Beaten by the Six Tenants.

7

$\mathcal{W}$hat did I do wrong?
Every day it gets harder.
I sit here blubbering all the time,
Telling myself I'm going to get out
Of this place, I've had it with this life.
The Lord of Death, a good servant,
Came in and spun the great wheel.
So I say to myself that I'm getting out of here
To spend what's left of my life reciting
Your name, but Kālī, You've got me so hooked
To the things of this world, I can't cut loose.

Rāmprasād cries at Kālī's feet:
O my dark Devī, I move through the shadows
Of Your world in a black mood.

8

$\mathscr{I}$t's this hope in hope, this happening again
To be in the world, this being over and over,
The bee's blunder when it goes for
The painted version of the lotus.

You've given me bitter leaves,
Swearing they were sweet, and my old
Sweet tooth has cost me a whole day
Spitting the bitterness out.

Mother, You lured me into this world,
You said: "Let's play," only to cheat
My hope out of its hope with Your playing.

Rāmprasād says: In this game
The end was a foregone conclusion.
Now, at dusk, take up Your child
In Your arms and go home.

9

_H_ow many times, Mother, are you going
To trundle me on this wheel like a blind-
Folded ox grinding out oil? You've got me
Tied to this old trunk of a world, flogging me
On and on. What have I done to be forced to serve
These Six Oily Dealers, the Passions?
All these births—eighty times 100,000—
As beast and bird and still the door
Of the womb is not shut on me
And I come out hurting once more!
When a child cries out, calling the precious name
Of mother, then a mother takes it in her arms.
Everywhere I look I see that's the rule,
Except for me. All some sinners need to do
Is shout "Durgā" and—pouf!—they're saved.

Take this blindfold off so I can see
The feet that give comfort. There are many
Bad children, but who ever heard
Of a bad mother?

There's only one hope
For Rāmprasād, Mother—that in the end
He will be safe at Your feet.

10

I'm sweating like the slave of an evil spirit,
Flat broke, a coolie working for nothing,
A ditch digger, and my body eats the profits.
Five Elements, Six Passions, Ten Senses—
Count them—all scream for attention.
They won't listen. I'm done for.
A blind man clutches the cane he's lost
Like a fanatic. So I clutch You, Mother,
But with my bungled karma, can't hold on.

Prasād cries out: Mother, cut this black snarl
Of acts, cut through it. Let life, when death
Closes down, shoot rejoicing up
Out of my head like a rocket.

11

*J*ust think of it, Mind—
No one's anything to anyone.

You've come back to this world
For nothing.

And for the few days of your life
They all call you master.

But they'll drop that master soon enough
When the master of life and death shows up.

And will she you worried yourself sick for,
Will she stick by you then?

The dear woman will sprinkle cow dung
To clear out the bad luck.

Shrī Rāmprasād says: When Death
Grabs you by the hair,
Call out: Kālī, Kālī—
Then what can He do?

12

*W*ho's with you, Mind,
And what are you waiting for?

Your poor tub of a body
Is grinding on the world's sand bar.

Move, move!—hoist the sail
With your guru's name and shove off.

Prasād says: Six Passions and all,
Shove off or darkness is going to bear down
And take you amidship.

13

So I say: Mind, don't you sleep
Or Time is going to get in and steal from you.

You hold on to the sword of Kālī's name.
The shield of Tārā's name.

Can Death overwhelm you?
Sound Kālī's name on a horn and sound it loud.

Chant "Durgā, Durgā,"
Until you bring the dawn around.

If She won't save you in this Dark Age—.
But how many great sinners have been saved!

Is Rāmprasād then
So unsalvageable a rogue?

14

I'm sick of living, Mother, sick.
Life and money have run out
But I go on crying "Tārā, Tārā,"
Hoping. You are the mother of all
And our nurse. You carry the Three Worlds
In Your belly.

So am I some orphan fallen out
Of the sky? And if You think I'm bad,
Remember, You're the cord connecting
Every good and evil
And I'm a tool tied to illusion.

Your name can blot out the fear
Of Death—so Shiva said,
But, Terrible One, You forget all that,
Absorbed in Shiva, Death, and Time.

Prasād says: Your games, Mother,
Are mysteries. You make and break.
You've broken me in this life.

15

Mother, tell me where I should stand
With no relations in this world?
The father loves a child loved
By the mother—that's well known.

But the Father who bears Stepmother
On His head—don't expect love from Him.
And if You aren't loving, why shouldn't I go
To Stepmother and if She takes me up
You won't see me around here anymore.

Rāmprasād says: Mother,
It's right there in the Vedas and Tantras:
He who repeats
Your name is going to end up
With a beggar's bowl and a cast-off rug.

16

$\mathcal{I}$'ve got a bone to pick with you, Mother.
You've trapped me in a family
And seen to it I stay poor.

You picked on Shiva too because He begged.
The best ritual, no doubt, is knowledge,
But charity is better than ritual.

Mother, Rādhā didn't go empty-handed
To Mathurā. You only pretend to be poor
Smearing Your skin with ashes.

So where is Your fortune? I know You've got
The Lord of Wealth in Your pocket.
Why do You hold out on Rāmprasād?

At Your feet I can defeat
Every evil every foot of the way.

17

*G*o on—I know You, Mother, I know You.
Who ever praises You and makes You hymns
Gets punished twice as hard for his trouble,
Gets roasted with pain and misery.

Nothing comes easy. It takes sweat
To hold back a flood, takes a strong man
To force his freedom out of You,
Takes a finger in Your eye
To get a little justice.

Mother, You gave those feet that Shiva worshipped
To Mahishāsura out of terror.
If somebody can tell You off,
If somebody comes armed,
You'll protect him always.

Rāmprasād wants only Your blessing
To be happy. So take every sense
But his voice so he can worship
At the feet of the dark Devī.

18

$\mathcal{W}$ho can explain Your play, Mother?
What do You take, what give back?
You give and take again.

For You dawn and dusk are the same.
Nothing can stop Your perfect freedom.
You give exactly what's deserved.

Even Shiva
Under Your feet, forgets
Your great design.

I see what You show me—a stone
Floating on water.
Rāmprasād is Your son;
He can see right through those old ploys.

19

You think motherhood is child's play?
One child doesn't make a mother if she's cruel.
Mine carried me ten months and ten days
But doesn't notice where I've gone
   when it's time to eat.

When a child is bad, his parents correct him,
But You can watch Death come at me
With murder in His heart
And turn away yawning.

Rāmprasād asks: Who taught You to be so cold?
If You want to be like Your father—
Stone—don't call Yourself
The Mother.

20

Mind, you gambled
And lost everything
So how do I move now?

My five best chessmen
Have led me on
And now there's my minister trembling,
Exposed on that pawn's square
And my horses hang back
And my elephant—why?
And my ships, laden with salt,
Sails set, lie idle at the dock
Though the wind is fair.

Rāmprasād says: so that's that.
And, look—it's check-mate
In my back row.

21

$\mathcal{M}$other, this beat-up shack
Is where I live and in my fear
I call You. Winds shake it
But Your name holds it up.
Every night the Six Thieves
Climb the mud wall and break in.
I can't fight them, so I run,
Mother, because Prasād confesses
That he doesn't want to be
A prisoner in his own house.

22

$\mathcal{H}$ow are You going to escape me?

This time—says the wretch—
I'm going to watch closely.

You'd snatch the fruit out of the hand
Of a child, eat it, Mother, and cheat him.

I'm going to hide mine so well
You can search all over and not find it.

You will run after me then
As the calf runs after the cow for milk.

Prasād says: find a half-wit
And fool him if You want,
But if You don't save me
I'm going to get Shiva to spank You.

23

$\mathcal{I}$'m not calling You
Anymore, crazy Kālī.

You, only a girl, waving a big sword,
Went into battle and without a stitch.

And there's that pittance You gave me
Only to snatch it right back.

As for this half-wit son,
You spoiled him all right, Mother.

Poor Rāmprasād cries:
Look what You've done Mother—
Piled this old tub
Full of goods, then sunk it.

24

I'm not calling you Mother anymore,
All You give me is trouble.
I had a home and a family, now
I'm a beggar—what will You think of
Next, my wild-haired Devī?

I'll beg before I come to You,
Crying "Mother." I've tried that
And got the silent treatment.
If the mother lives should the son suffer,
And if she's dead, hasn't he got to live somehow?

Rāmprasād says: What's a mother
Anyway, the son's worst enemy?
I keep wondering what worse You can do
Than make me live over and over
The pain, life after life.

25

Somehow the time will pass.
Today is going to pass,
Only Your story will live,
Your name, Tārā, dirtied by Your cruelty.
I came here to this marketplace
And, sold out, wait at the landing.
Mother, the sun is dying. I need a boat,
And this boatman takes only those who can pay.
He demands money
But where will a poor man get it?

Prasād cries: Woman of Stone,
Glance back and give me a seat.
I'm going to plunge anyway, singing
Your greatness, into the sea of this world.

26

You sleep on in that sleep of desire,
Found yourself a fine bed
Of Time in this worldly world.
You think there's no dawn in this night
Of pleasure? Your old mistress Lust
Lies by you and you're too lazy to turn
Away from her, pulling Hope like a sheet
Over your head, hiding your face—
Like this winter and summer, refusing
To send the sheet to the wash. You've drunk
The wine of this world and can't stop drinking,
Day and night drunk and don't even cry,
Without thinking, Kālī's name.

You utter idiot, Prasād, Hope
Isn't satisfied while you're asleep
And in this sleep a deeper sleep
Will come when you won't wake
    though called and called.

27

*M*ind, you just stay awake crying:
"Hurrah for Kālī! Hurrah for Kālī!"
Don't you dare sleep, you nitwit,
And lose your fortune.
                        When you lie
Snoring comfortably, there are nine doors
To come through for those Passionate Villains
Who are out to steal your goods.

𝒟oes suffering scare me? O Mother,
Let me suffer in this world. Do I require more?
Suffering runs ahead of me and runs after me.
I carry it on my head and set up a stand
In the bazaar to peddle it.
I'm a poison worm, I thrive on poison.
I carry it wherever I go.

Prasād says: Mother, lift off my load.
I need a little rest. It's amazing!
Others brag about their happiness,
I brag about my suffering.

29

*I*s there yet
Another saving ritual from the Vedas?

My reputation is gone.
All I've got left is this bad name.

It's all drudgery, drudgery—
Birth and death polluting my works.

First, my wife, who is called Thought,
Was barren. Then, after loving,

Bore me a son
By the name of Bliss-in-Knowledge.

My selfish father simply ran off,
Indifferent to the world. Māyā, my mother, died.

Sickness and Sorrow were my brothers,
One a miser, the other open-handed.

Two sisters I had, Hunger and Thirst.
No one ever had a good word for me.

Prasād says: Why live
In so threatening a house? I'll take these few things—
The sort Shiva carries—and singing:
"Hurrah for Kālī," I'll just dance off.

30

O Mother, who really
Knows Your magic?

You're a crazy girl
Driving us all crazy with these tricks.

No one knows anyone else
In a world of Your illusions.

Kālī's tricks are so deft,
We act on what we see.

And what suffering—
All because of a crazy girl!

Who knows
What She truly is?

Rāmprasād says: If She decides
To be kind, this misery will pass.

31

She's no ordinary girl, my Umā.
She's not Your daughter, Lord of the Mountain.
I swear she's not. I'm afraid
To tell you, Lord, what I dreamt:
That Umā's was the face of the God with Four Faces
And the God with Five Faces. She was the Great Devī
Smiling as She spoke. Vishṇu came,
The Dark One, riding Garuḍa,
His hands pleadingly clasped.

Prasād says: O lucky Lord,
How do You rate a daughter
Whom even the holy can't approach?

O Giri, I can't comfort
Your Umā anymore.

She cries and pouts,
Won't take the breast,
Won't touch Her *khir*,
And shoves away Her cream.

When the moon lifts
In the night sky
She begs me to get
The moon for Her.

Her eyes are swollen,
Her face pale—
How can a mother
Stand it!

Crying, "Come, Mother,
Come," She holds my little finger,
Wanting to go
I don't know where.

I ask Her—"Is there any way
To get the moon?"
And She flings
Her jewelry at me.

Giri sits up, lovingly
Takes Gaurī on His lap

And smiling says: "Little mother, here
Is the moon," handing Her a mirror.

Seeing Her face in the glass
She's happy,
And so shames
A million moons.

Shrī Rāmprasād says: He's a rich man
In whose house the Mother lives,
And, saying this, he lays Her down
In Her small bed, fast asleep.

33

My life's lord, Giri, my husband,
   Look at me tremble!
What's this terrible story I hear?—
   Darkness in broad day.
                     There Shiva sits
On his tiger skin by our door crying
Again and again: "Come out, Mother
Of Gaṇesh, come out!"
                     You must have a heart
Of Rock, my stony man, or else
It would have split by now.
                     Our daughter
Is another's property—my heart knows
But can't quite grasp it.
                     O, the bitterness
Of it, this shocking play of Providence!

Prasād says this to you:
                     Himālaya
And His queen are like *chakorī* birds
At dawn—starved for moonbeams.

34

*C*he dark Mother
Is flying a kite
In the world's fairground.

O, mind, see—you are up there
In the gusts of hope,
Payed out on the string of illusion,
Your frame strung together
Skeleton and pulse stuck on.

But the Maker overdid it,
Giving the kite too much ego
In the building,
Toughening the string with glue
And powdered glass.

So Mother, if out of a thousand kites
You lose one or two,
Laugh and clap.

Prasād says: that kite is going to take off
In the southern breeze,
And on the other shore
Of this ocean of lives
It will dive fast to its freedom.

35

About maya
This is the strangest of all—

Those trapped in it
Scurry every which way.

Those free of it
Rest contented.

"I'm this. This is mine."
Idiot thoughts.

O Mind, you imagined all that stuff was real
And carelessly tangled the heart!

"Who am I? Who is mine?
Who else is real?"

O Mind, who serves and who is the served?
All this gladness and sadness are nothing.

O Mind, the light in a dark room
Is snuffed by possessions.

Everything finally is lost
So live in a wise house and be wary.

Rāmprasād says:
Lift the mosquito net and look at yourself.

36

*W*hat's so good in You
That You deserve to be called Mother?

The sad and the injured
Revile You.

Because of You, Mother, Father is crazy,
With Stepmother sitting on His head.

The old man can't understand.
He wears Himself out repeating Durgā, Durgā.

Not even His father has the power,
As You have, to provide with ten hands.

Why, Tārā, do You
Always save hot words for Him?

You've perished a hundred times,
And Shiva goes around with bones for a necklace.

Twice-born Rāmprasād says: people mock me.
They say: "If your mother is Annapūrṇā,
Why isn't there food in your father's house?"

37

*K*ālī, why are You naked again?
Good grief, haven't You any shame?

Mother, don't You have clothes?
Where is the pride of a king's daughter?

And, Mother, is this some family duty—
This standing on the chest of Your man?

You're naked, He's naked,
You hang around the burning grounds.

O, Mother, we are dying of shame.
Now put on Your woman's clothes.

Mother, Your necklace gleams,
Those human heads shine at Your throat.

Prasād says: Even Shiva fears You
When You're like this.

38

*A*ll right, You crazy woman,
Get down off the Great Lord's chest!

Shiva's not dead; He's simply
The Master Yogī meditating.

But poison has weakened Him,
He can't bear the force of Your feet, Mother.

Now, get down before His ribs cave in—
O Shiva's Woman, You're pitiless, pitiless.

He drank poison and survived,
Why should He die now?

Rāmprasād thinks He's playing dead
Just to have Your feet touching Him.

I'm dazed thinking about it—
How can five lunatics live together?
Mother's crazy, Father—He's crazy,
So are His two attendants,
And I'm going half crazy myself,
Brooding, Mother, on Your saving feet.

Has anyone before seen a man so mad?
Putting Her feet on His lotus heart,
This same fellow who leaves golden Kāshī
To live in the burning grounds.

And who'll listen if I tell what it's like
To live in such a household?—Like pot, like pan.

Is there anyone else like this girl
Wearing a necklace of chopped off heads?

Prasād says: I don't know what
It's all about, so do what You have to,
But shake me loose from this fear of death.

40

*M*other, how many times do I have to say this?
I'm a draggle of seaweed in a flood of misery.
Sex (at my age!), anger, greed, lethargy,
Pride, envy—all tugging at all times
Every which way on this old body and it hurts.

Twice-born Rāmprasād has got to say
That, Mother, You've forgotten all
About pity. Just come down once
And stand in this lotus heart,
Let me see You once and for all.

41

What am I—a rickety thing
Born a month early?

I'm not giving You up
No matter how you glare at me.

What's all this teasing and tricks, Mother,
When I go to get what's mine?

I've got Shiva's promissory note
Signed and sealed in my heart.

Now I'm going to take You to His court
And get a ruling.

I'll show You what kind of son You've got
When the hearing begins.

I've also got the deed of my guru
To show the court.

Rāmprasād says: this trial between us
Is going to be a beauty, Mother.
And I'm not going to settle
Unless You take me lovingly to You.

42

$\mathcal{I}$'ve got You figured, Hara—
I'm going to grab Mother's feet and hang on.

Bholānātha has slipped up this time
And I'm telling everybody and anybody.

How can He, a father, keep holding
Mother's feet to His heart?

As soon as father and son meet
I'm going to put it to Him.

He stole Mother's feet.
Does He think He's fooling anyone, playing dead?

A child inherits his mother's wealth—
How does He explain taking it from me?

If Bholā wants what's right
He'd better let those feet go.

I'm going to tell the world about Him,
Even though it's my own father.

Rāmprasād says: I'm not scared.
Those feet trample fear.

43

*C*ome on, Mind, let's go steal—
You and I together—
All Shiva owns—Mother's feet,
If we can carry them off.

But if they catch us
In that watchful house,
That would be the end of the body.
They'd tie us up in Kailāsa.

Don't forget your guru's advice
If we get in; we'll wound Shiva
With an arrow of devotion,
Then grab those feet and run.

44

$\mathcal{G}$o on with the deception—
I'm not going to be fooled anymore.

I've come to rest at these calming feet,
So the fear and trembling are over.

I'm light, light of the Passions
That almost sank me in the poisoned well.

Pleasure and pain—what's the difference?
The uncontrollable fire in my head is going out.

No more of the wine of desire,
No more drunken begging door to door.

No more snatching at windy hope,
No more loose talk from the heart.

I'm through with the tangling dazzle of tricks,
And through with swings on the tree of love.

Rāmprasād says: It's the pure milk I tasted,
Why add buttermilk?

45

*M*ind, why do you fret so much,
Like a motherless child?

Here you are hunched up
Continually brooding on Death.

The Great Death can handle that
And He's under the Mother's feet.

A snake afraid of a frog?—what rubbish!
Can you, your Mother's son, fear Death?

You're mad—is anyone whose mother
Is the Mother afraid of Death?

Why do you sit in there crushed
When all you have to say is "Durgā, Durgā"?

Fear departs when you wake up.
That's the way it will be.

Twice-born Rāmprasād says: Mind,
You do what you want,
Keep on following the guru's word,
And what can He do, this Death
Though He's the Son of the Sun?

46

Now cry Kālī and take the plunge!
O, my Mind, dive into this sea,
This heart which has yet to be sounded.
There are gems down there that two or three dives
Aren't going to get. Now, hold your breath
And jump! Kick down to where She sits
Deep in the wise waters, a great pearl.
You can do it, all it takes
Is overwhelming love and the memory
Of Shiva's good words.

Down there the Six Passions cruise
Like crocodiles snapping at anything
That moves, so cover yourself with knowledge
Like turmeric smeared on the skin—
The odor will keep them off.
I tell you there's a world of wealth
In that water.

Rāmprasād says: Dive in
And you're going to come up with a fortune.

47

I've given my heart
To the feet that forestall terror—
What have I got to fear from Death?

Kālī's name is the wish-giving tree.
My heart is seeded with it.

I've peddled my bones in the marketplace
Of this world and bought up Durgā's name.

I'm rooming in the house
Of the good soul living in this flesh.

So when Death enters, I've made up my mind
To open my heart, to show Him all.

Tārā's name is the best remedy.
I've tied it to my topknot.

Rāmprasād says: I have begun
My journey calling on the name
Of Durgā.

48

*G*o on—you're only Death's flunky,
But I'm Mother's son.

You go ask your lord
How many like me
He's welcomed warmly.

I can be the death
Of Death if only
I keep Her light steady in my mind.

Prasād says: listen, lackey,
You watch your mouth around here.
If you're tied up in Kālī's name
And beaten, who's going to save you?

49

You'd better not touch me,
Death—I've just lost caste
On the very day
The kind Mother was kind to me.

Listen, Death,
And I'll tell You how I lost it:
I was a family man
And that Dark Destroyer
Made me a beggar.
My heart and tongue joined forces
To sing Kālī's name,
And the Six Passions,
Hearing that, jumped overboard
And swam off.

The power that made me an outcaste
Is still wholly here.

Prasād says:
When an outcast dies,
Let Death not come too near.

50

*A*ll right, Death,
Here I am.

I've drawn a circle around me
With Kālī's name.

The Great Death, Kālī on His chest,
Has taken Her feet to His heart.

Remembering that Her feet
Cancel all fear,
Who needs to fear Death?

51

What's more to fear
Around this place?

My body is Tārā's field
In which the God of Gods
Like a good farmer
Sows His seed with a great *mantra*.

Around this body, faith
Is set like a fence
With patience for posts.

With Shiva watching
What can the thieves of time
Hope to do?

He oversees the Six Oxen
Driving them out of the barn.

He mows the grass of sin
With the honed blade of Kālī's name.

Love rains down
And Devotion night and day.

Prasād says: On Kālī's tree
Goodness, wealth, love and release
Can be had for the picking.

52

You'll find Mother
In any house.

Do I dare say it in public?

She is Bhairavī with Shiva,
Durgā with Her children,
Sītā with Lakshmaṇa.

She's mother, daughter, wife, sister—
Every woman close to you.

What more can Rāmprasād say?
You work the rest out from these hints.

53

My mind dreams up this image
I could make with clay.
But is Mother clay?
It's a waste of labor.
She has a sword, a necklace of skulls.
Is Mother then an image of clay?
Can an image of clay
Cool the mind's fever?
I've heard the hue of Her skin is a dark
That lights the world.
Can an image of clay be made
That marvelous dark with a coat of paint?
And Mother's eyes
Are the sun, the moon, the fire.
What craftsman can render such eyes?
Kālī cuts down evil.
Is this the work of straw and clay?

She will scour his mind
And show Herself to Rāmprasād.

54

*W*hy should I go to Kāshī?
At Her feet you'll find it all—
Gayā, the Ganges, Kāshī.
Meditating in my lotus heart
I float on blissful waters.
Her feet are red lotuses
Crammed with shrines
And Her name spoken
Consumes evil like a fire
In a pile of dry cotton.
If there is no head to worry,
You can't have a headache.

Everytime I hear about Gayā,
The offerings there, the good deeds
Recited, I laugh. I know Shiva
Has said that dying at Kāshī saves.
But I know too that salvation
Always follows worship around
Like a slave, and what's this salvation
If it swallows the saved like water
In water? Sugar I love
But haven't the slightest desire
To merge with sugar.

Rāmprasād says with amazement:
Grace and mercy in Her wild hair—
Think of that
And all good things are yours.

55

Q Mind, do you still cherish this fantasy of yours?
What is Kālī that you stare and haven't seen Her?
O, you know the Three Worlds
    are the Mother's image,
You know, but do you really believe it?
What kind of thing is your heart
    that it makes Her likeness
In clay and then offers it up prayers?

56

She's playing in my heart.
Whatever I think, I think Her name.
I close my eyes and She's in there
Garlanded with human heads.

Common sense, know-how—gone,
So they say I'm crazy. Let them.
All I ask, my crazy Mother,
Is that You stay put.

Rāmprasād cries out: Mother, don't
Reject this lotus heart You live in,
Don't despise this human offering
At Your feet.

57

*W*hy go live by the Ganges?

I'm going to sit here
And chant Mother's name.

Why leave home
And live somewhere else?

At Her feet I have
Hundreds of Ganges and Gayās.

Rāmprasād says:
There's shelter enough
At Kālī's feet.
I'm not the kind of a son
Who calls a stepmother
Mother.

58

*M*other, incomparably arrayed,
Hair flying, stripped down,
You battle-dance on Shiva's heart,
A garland of heads that bounce off
Your heavy hips, chopped-off hands
For a belt, the bodies of infants
For earrings, and the lips,
The teeth like jasmine, the face
A lotus blossomed, the laugh,
And the dark body boiling up and out
Like a storm cloud, and those feet
Whose beauty is only deepened by blood.

So Prasād cries: My mind is dancing!
Can I take much more? Can I bear
An impossible beauty?

59

Sing Kālī's glory,
Make a happy racket,
Paddle this old boat of a body
As fast as you can.

What's the trouble
Of this world anyhow?

Hoist your mind
To catch the wind.
Death can just stand on the shore
And gape as you go spanking by,
Sail full of the southern breeze.

Shiva's no liar—
He'll make all these powers
Over which He has power
Yours.

Prasād says: anyone
Who doesn't agree
Can just get out.

60

What good is a trip to Kāshī?
Right here at Kālī's feet you can find
All ways out of this world.
Right at Her feet there are three hundred
And fifty million holy places for worship.

If you know the prayer,
If you understand the good words,
Why do you have to set up house at Kāshī?

Think of the four-armed Kālī
And that flying hair
In your lotus heart.

O Rāmprasād, sitting tight
In this same room, you will be,
Day and night, in Kāshī.

61

Shout Her name: Kālī, Kālī!
If they say, "He's an old crackpot,"
Let them. If they say bad things
About you, what's it to you?
Good is one thing, evil another.
It's good to be doing good.
With Her name you can hack your way
Through all this junk, the trash of a lifetime.

But, O Rāmprasād, admit it—
You still walk through this sweet sham
Of a world heartsick, dazed.

62

That's it, Mother!
The play is done.
It's over, my Happy One.
I came into this world
To play, took the dust
Of this world and played,
And now, Daughter of High Places,
Suddenly I'm scared. Death is so near,
So serious. I think of those games
I played as a boy, and all that breath
Wasted in the pleasure of marriage
When it should have gone for prayer.

Rāmprasād begs: Mother,
Old age has broken me—what do I do now?
Mother, teach this worshipper
Worship, plunge me
Into the saving waters.

APPENDIX

We have drawn upon four Bengali collections for the lyrics in this book: *Rāmprasād Sener Granthābalī*, 6th ed. (Calcutta: Basumati-Sahitya-Mandir, n.d.); Amarendranath Ray, ed., *Shākta Padābalī* (Calcutta: Calcutta University, 1957); Yogendranath Gupta, *Sādhak Kabi Rāmprasād* (Calcutta: Bhattacharya Sons, Ltd., 1954); and Kamal Kumar Gangopadhyay, ed., *Shākta-pada Sāhitya o Shākta-padābalī Cayan* (Calcutta: M. L. De & Co., n.d.). Many of the lyrics have already been translated into English and French in the following volumes: Edward J. Thompson and Arthur Marshman Spencer, *Bengali Religious Lyrics*, Sakta (Calcutta: Oxford University Press, 1923); Jadunath Sinha, *Rama Prasada's Devotional Songs* (Calcutta: Sinha Publishing House Pvt. Ltd., 1966); and Michèle Lupsa, *Chants à Kālī de Rāmprasād* (Pondicherry: Institut Français d'Indologie, 1967).

1. RSG: 133	9. SKR: 203	17. RSG: 226
2. RSG: 7	10. SP: 167	18. SKR: 132
3. RSG: 223	11. RSG: 111	19. RSG: 52
4. RSG: (Addenda) 28	12. RSG: 41	20. RSG: 135
5. RSG: 120	13. SP: 288	21. RSG: 27
6. RSG: 4	14. SKR: 253	22. SKR: 97
7. RSG: 146	15. RSG: 130	23. RSG: 18
8. SP: 157	16. RSG: 172	24. RSG: 43

25. RSG: 224	38. RSG: (Addenda) 64	51. SKR: 34
26. SP: 233	39. SKR: 252	52. RSG: 15
27. RSG: 70	40. SKR: 213	53. SP: 103
28. RSG: 137	41. SP: 314	54. SP: 332
29. SKR: 87	42. SP: 312	55. SSSC: 1
30. RSG: 20	43. RSG: 176	56. RSG: 88
31. SP: 1	44. SP: 313	57. RSG: 42
32. SP: 2	45. SP: 253	58. RSG: 187
33. SP: 97	46. SP: 264	59. RSG: 222
34. SP: 271	47. SKR: 6	60. SP: 335
35. RSG: 166	48. RSG: 57	61. RSG: 96
36. SKR: 89	49. SKR: 10	62. RSG: 16
37. SKR: 79	50. RSG: 14	

GLOSSARY

Annapūrṇā: she who is full [*pūrṇā*] with food [*anna*]; an epithet for the goddess as the munificent provider.

Bhairavī: the goddess; *see* Introduction.

Bholānātha: the forgetful [*bholā*] lord [*nātha*]; an epithet for Shiva who, under the influence of the narcotic *gāñjā* and because he is often in a meditative (yogic) trance, is frequently forgetful of his duties.

chakorī: birds supposed to feed on moonbeams; feminine of *chakora*.

Dark Age: *kali*, the last of the four *yugas* or ages within the Hindu cosmic cycle; other *yugas* in order of occurrence are *krita* (also known as *satya*), *tretā*, and *dvāpara*; the *kali yuga*, in which we now live, is the most degenerate of the four and ends with the destruction of the universe which will then be recreated anew.

Dark Destroyer: an epithet for the goddess as destroyer.

Dark One: an epithet for Vishṇu.

Daughter of the High Places: an epithet for the goddess whose father is the high mountains, the Himālayas; *see* Giri or Himālaya.

Devī: "goddess"; as Durgā or Kālī, her iconography shows her to have a third eye (as does Shiva) in the middle of her forehead; feminine of *deva* [god].

Durgā: the goddess; *see* Introduction.

69

Five Elements: earth, water, fire, air, and ether.

Five Senses: *see* Ten Senses.

Gaṇesh: lord [*ish*, from *ishvara*] of the people or demigods [*gaṇas*]; the elephant-headed son of Shiva and the goddess.

Ganges: the river which runs from the Himālayas through north-central India, emptying into the Bay of Bengal; this celestial river goddess descended to earth, falling first on Shiva's matted hair so as not to crush the world on impact; she is considered the second wife of Shiva, co-wife with Durgā, and thus stepmother to the poet; the Ganges, being sacred, is a place of pilgrimage.

Garuḍa: a mythical, giant bird that transports Vishṇu.

Gaurī: the goddess; *see* Introduction.

Gayā: a sacred place of pilgrimage in northeastern India.

Giri: "mountain"; the name of the goddess's father; *see* Himālaya.

God of Gods: an epithet for Shiva.

God with Five Faces: an epithet for Shiva whose iconography sometimes shows him with five faces.

God with Four Faces: an epithet for Brahmā whose iconography sometimes shows him with four faces.

Great Death: an epithet for Shiva who brings about the destruction of the universe at the end of the *kali yuga*.

Great Lord: an epithet for Shiva.

guru: a guide-teacher in spiritual matters.

Happy One: an epithet for the goddess as she who is full of *ānanda* [bliss].

Hara: "destroyer"; an epithet for Shiva.

Hari: a name of Vishṇu; when a Bengali Hindu dies, relatives and friends, chanting Hari's name bear the shrouded body (face exposed) to the burning ground for cremation on a litter adorned with flowers and incense; a pitcher is used to pour sacred water on the ashes.

Himālaya: abode [*ālaya*] of snow [*hima*]; the name of the goddess's father; the northern mountain range in the South Asian subcontinent; *see* Giri.

Kailāsa: a mountain in the Himālayas on top of which live Shiva and his goddess wife.

Kālī: the goddess; *see* Introduction.

karma: action; "fate," acts whose consequences affect the actor now and/or in a subsequent life.

Kāshī: another name for Benares, a city most sacred to Shiva.

khir: milk boiled down until thick, with sugar added.

Lakshmaṇa: brother-in-law to Sītā.

Lord of the Mountain: an epithet for the goddess's father; *see* Giri or Himālaya.

Mahishāsura: water-buffalo [*mahisha*] demon or antigod [*asura*]; slain by Durgā.

mantra: a special, sacred utterance.

Mathurā: Krishṇa's birthplace in north-central India.

Māyā: "illusion," what seems real to man; one of the powers all-mighty divinities possess and a deified power in her own right.

Rādhā: lover of Krishṇa; she was forced to pay the boatman (Krishṇa in disguise) before he would take her to Mathurā.

Shiva: a supreme god in Hinduism, the gods' god; his two attendants are Nandi and Bhriṇgi; *see* Introduction.

Sītā: wife of Rāma and sister-in-law to his younger brother, Lakshmaṇa.

Six Passions, etc.: lust, anger, greed, lethargy, pride, and envy, the enemies [*ripu*] of man; *see* Introduction.

Son of the Sun: an epithet for Yama, lord of death; the Sun's other son is the malevolent planet Saturn [*shani*].

Stepmother: *see* Ganges.

Tantras: texts pertinent to Shaktism; sacred books of a tradition not of but parallel to that contained in the Vedas; *see* Vedas.

Tārā: the goddess; *see* Introduction.

Ten Senses: the "senses" of action [*karmendriya*] are (1) speech organ [*vāk*], (2) hand [*pāṇi*], (3) foot [*pada*], (4) anus [*pāyu*], and genitalia [*upastha*]; the "senses" of knowledge [*jñānendriya*] are (1) eye [*cakshu*], (2) ear [*karṇa*], (3) nose [*nāsikā*], (4) tongue [*jīhvā*], and skin [*tvak*].

Terrible One: an epithet for the goddess as fear-instiller.

Three Worlds: heaven [*svarga*], "mortal" earth [*martya*], and the nether world [*pātāla*]; collectively, the entire universe.

Twice-born: a term designating, theoretically, a member of any of the higher *varṇas* (Brāhman, Kshatriya, or Vaishya) after ritual rebirth through the *upanayana* ceremony during which the sacred thread is vested; usually refers to a Brāhman, also spelled Brāhmin; Bengali Vaidyas may claim twice-born status.

Vedas: the most ancient sacred books of the Hindus.

Vishṇu: a supreme god in Hinduism; he is dark complexioned.

Umā: the goddess; *see* Introduction.

Woman of Stone: an epithet for the goddess whose father is the stone mountains, the Himālayas; *see* Giri or Himālaya.

Yogī: one who practices yoga; Shiva is the greatest of *yogis; see* Introduction.

ADDITIONAL TITLES FROM HOHM PRESS

RENDING THE VEIL: Literal and Poetic Translations of Rumi
by Shahram T. Shiva   Preface by Peter Lamborn Wilson

With a groundbreaking transliteration, English-speaking lovers of Rumi's poetry will have the opportunity to "read" his verse aloud, observing the rhythm, the repetition, and the rhyme that Rumi himself used over 800 years ago. Offers the reader a hand at the magical art of translation, providing a unique word-by-word literal translation from which to compose one's own variations. Together with exquisitely-rendered Persian calligraphy of 252 of Rumi's quatrains (many previously untranslated), Mr. Shiva presents his own poetic English version of each piece. From his study of more than 2000 of Rumi's short poems, the translator presents a faithful cross-section of the poet's many moods, from fierce passion to silent adoration.

"Faithfully polished translations." – *Publisher's Weekly*

Cloth, 280 pages, $27.95   ISBN: 0-934252-46-7

• • •

FOR LOVE OF THE DARK ONE: SONGS OF MIRABAI
Revised edition
Translations and Introduction by Andrew Schelling

Mirabai is probably the best known poet in India today, even though she lived 400 years ago (1498-1593). Her poems are ecstatic declarations of surrender to and praise of Krishna, whom she lovingly calls "The Dark One." Mira's poetry is as alive today as it was in the sixteenth century—a poetry of freedom, of breaking with traditional stereotypes, of trusting completely in the benediction of God. It is also some of the most exalted mystical poetry in all of world literature, expressing her complete surrender to the Divine, her longing, and her madness in love. This revised edition contains the original 80 poems, a completely revised Introduction, updated glossary, bibliography and discography, and additional Sanskrit notations.

Paper, 128 pages, $12.00   ISBN: 0-934252-84-X

**TO ORDER PLEASE SEE ACCOMPANYING ORDER FORM
OR CALL 1-800-381-2700 TO PLACE YOUR ORDER NOW.**

ADDITIONAL TITLES FROM HOHM PRESS

FACETS OF THE DIAMOND: THE WISDOM OF INDIA
by James Capellini

Anyone who has ever felt the pull of India's spiritual heritage will find a treasure in this book. Contains rare photographs, brief biographic sketches and evocative quotes from contemporary spiritual teachers representing India's varied spiritual paths—from pure Advaita Vedanta (non-dualism) to the Hindu Vaisnava (Bhakti) devotional tradition. Highlights such well-known sages as Ramana Maharshi, Nityananda, and Shirdi Sai Baba, as well as many renowned saints who are previously unknown in the West.

Text in three languages—English, French and German

Cloth, 224 pages, $39.95, 42 b&w photographs   ISBN: 0-934252-53-X

• • •

THE YOGA TRADITION: Its History, Literature, Philosophy and Practice
by Georg Feuerstein, Ph.D.
Foreword by Ken Wilber

A complete overview of the great Yogic traditions of Raja-Yoga, Hatha-Yoga, Jnana-Yoga, Bhakti-Yoga, Karma-Yoga, Tantra-Yoga, Kundalini-Yoga, Mantra-Yoga and many other lesser known forms. Includes translations of over twenty famous Yoga treatises, like the *Yoga-Sutra of Patanjali*, and a first-time translation of the *Goraksha Paddhati*, an ancient Hatha Yoga text. Covers all aspects of Hindu, Buddhist, Jaina and Sikh Yoga. A necessary resource for all students and scholars of Yoga.

"Without a doubt the finest overall explanation of Yoga. Destined to become a classic." – Ken Wilber

Paper, 708 pages, over 200 illustrations, $39.95   ISBN: 0-934252-83-1

Cloth, $49.95   ISBN: 0-934252-88-2

TO ORDER PLEASE SEE ACCOMPANYING ORDER FORM
OR CALL 1-800-381-2700 TO PLACE YOUR ORDER NOW.

ADDITIONAL TITLES FROM HOHM PRESS

THE MIRROR OF THE SKY
Songs of the Bauls of Bengal
Translated by Deben Bhattacharya

Baul music today is prized by world musicologists, and Baul lyrics are
treasured by readers of ecstatic and mystical poetry. Baul music, lyrics,
and accompanying dance reflect the passion, the devotion and the
iconoclastic freedom of this remarkable sect of musicians and lovers of
the Divine, affectionately known as "God's troubadours."

The Mirror of the Sky is a translation of 204 songs, including an exten-
sive introduction to the history and faith of the Bauls, and the composition
of their music. It includes a CD of authentic Baul artists, recorded as much
as forty years ago by Bhattacharya, a specialist in world music. The current
CD is a rare presentation of this infrequently documented genre.

Paper, 288 pages, $24.95 (includes CD)   ISBN: 0-934252-89-0
CD sold separately, $16.95

• • •

CRAZY AS WE ARE
Selected Rubais from the Divan-i-Kebir of Mevlana Celaleddin Rumi

Introduction and Translation by Dr. Nevit O. Ergin

This book is a collection of 128 previously untranslated *rubais*, or
quatrains (four-line poems which express one complete idea), of the 13th-
century scholar and mystic poet Rumi. Filled with the passion of both
ecstasy and pain, Rumi's words may stir remembrance and longing, or
challenge complacency in the presence of awesome love. Ergin's
translations (directly from Farsi, the language in which Rumi wrote) are
fresh and highly sensitive, reflecting his own resonance with the path of
annihilation in the Divine as taught by the great Sufi masters.

Paper, 88 pages, $9.95   ISBN 0-934252-30-0

**TO ORDER PLEASE SEE ACCOMPANYING ORDER FORM
OR CALL 1-800-381-2700 TO PLACE YOUR ORDER NOW.**

ADDITIONAL TITLES FROM HOHM PRESS

THE WOMAN AWAKE: Feminine Wisdom for Spiritual Life
by Regina Sara Ryan

Through the stories and insights of great women of spirit whom the
author has met or been guided by in her own journey, this book high-
lights many faces of the Divine Feminine: the silence, the solitude, the
service, the power, the compassion, the art, the darkness, the sexuality.
Read about: the Sufi poetess Rabia (8th century) and contemporary Sufi
master Irina Tweedie; Hildegard of Bingen, Mechtild of Magdeburg, and
Hadewijch of Brabant: the Beguines of medieval Europe; author Kathryn
Hulme *(The Nun's Story)* who worked with Gurdjieff; German healer and
mystic Dina Rees...and many others.

Paper, 35 b&w photos; 520 pages, $19.95   ISBN: 0-934252-79-3

• • •

GRACE AND MERCY IN HER WILD HAIR
Selected Poems to the Mother Goddess
by Ramprasad Sen; Translated by Leonard Nathan and Clinton Seely

Ramprasad Sen, a great devotee of the Mother Goddess, composed these
passionate poems in 18th-century Bengal, India. His lyrics are songs of
praise or sorrowful laments addressed to the great goddesses Kali and
Tara, guardians of the cycles of birth and death.

Paper, 120 pages, $12.00   ISBN 0-934252-94-7

**TO ORDER PLEASE SEE ACCOMPANYING ORDER FORM
OR CALL 1-800-381-2700 TO PLACE YOUR ORDER NOW.**

ADDITIONAL TITLES FROM HOHM PRESS

IN PRAISE OF RUMI
by Lee Lozowick, and others   Introduction by Regina Sara Ryan

Once a great Turkish scholar and theologian, Jelaluddin Rumi lost his heart to a wandering beggar, Shams E Tabriz, in whom he saw the face of God. His poetry extols his love and longing—for his beloved teacher, and for the Divine, alive in all things. *In Praise of Rumi* is a book of ecstatic poetry. It is an expression from the same chamber of the heart in which Rumi danced over 700 years ago. A book for those who know what it means to have a wounded heart, *In Praise of Rumi* celebrates the bittersweet pain and pleasure of tasting the raw Divine.

Paper, 80 pages, $8.00   ISBN: 0-934252-23-8

**TO ORDER PLEASE SEE ACCOMPANYING ORDER FORM
OR CALL 1-800-381-2700 TO PLACE YOUR ORDER NOW.**

RETAIL ORDER FORM FOR HOHM PRESS BOOKS

Name_____ Phone (___) _____

Street Address or P.O. Box _____

City _____ State _____ Zip Code _____

QTY	TITLE	ITEM PRICE	TOTAL PRICE	
1	CRAZY AS WE ARE	$9.95		
2	FACETS OF THE DIAMOND	$39.95		
3	FOR LOVE OF THE DARK ONE	$12.00		
4	GRACE AND MERCY IN HER WILD HAIR	$12.00		
5	IN PRAISE OF RUMI	$8.00		
6	MIRROR OF THE SKY, INCLUDES CD	$24.95		
7	MIRROR OF THE SKY, CD ONLY	$16.95		
8	RENDING THE VEIL	$27.95		
9	THE WOMAN AWAKE	$19.95		
10	YOGA TRADITION, PAPER	$39.95		
11	YOGA TRADITION, CLOTH	$49.95		

SURFACE SHIPPING CHARGES

1st book $4.00

Each additional item $1.00

SUBTOTAL:

SHIPPING: (see below)

TOTAL:

SHIP MY ORDER

☐ Surface U.S. Mail—Priority   ☐ UPS (Mail + $2.00)

☐ 2nd-Day Air (Mail + $5.00)   ☐ Next-Day Air (Mail + $15.00)

METHOD OF PAYMENT:

☐ Check or M.O.   Payable to Hohm Press, P.O. Box 2501, Prescott, AZ 86302

☐ Call 1-800-381-2700 to place your credit card order

☐ Or call 1-520-717-1779 to fax your credit card order

☐ Information for Visa/MasterCard order only:

Card #_____–_____–_____–_____   Expiration Date _____

Visit our Website to view our complete catalog: www.hohmpress.com
ORDER NOW! Call 1-800-381-2700 or fax your order to 1-520-717-1779.
(Remember to include your credit card information.)